Drewett

CONTENTS

● **INTRODUCTION**   3

● **KNOW THE GAME**
THE COURT   4-5
EQUIPMENT   6-7

● **PREPARATION**
BODY POSITION   8-9
GRIPS   10-11
RULES OF PLAY   12-13
WARMING UP   14-15

● **THE STROKES**
FOREHAND STROKES   16-17
BACKHAND STROKES   18-19
ON THE COURT: GROUNDSTROKES   20-21
THE SERVE   22-23
ON THE COURT: THE SERVE   24-25
SERVICE RETURNS   26-27
ON THE COURT: SERVICE RETURNS   28-29
THE VOLLEY   30-31
ON THE COURT: THE VOLLEY   32-33

● **ADVANCED SKILLS**
THE LOB   34-35
ON THE COURT: THE LOB   36-37
THE SMASH   38-39
ON THE COURT: THE SMASH   40-41
THE DROP SHOT   42-43

● **BE FIT, STAY FIT**
DIET & MENTAL ATTITUDE   44-45

● **HOW THE FAMOUS DO IT**   46-47

● **GLOSSARY/LISTINGS**   48

● **INDEX**   Inside back cover

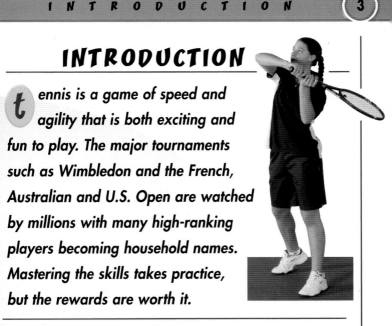

INTRODUCTION

t ennis is a game of speed and agility that is both exciting and fun to play. The major tournaments such as Wimbledon and the French, Australian and U.S. Open are watched by millions with many high-ranking players becoming household names. Mastering the skills takes practice, but the rewards are worth it.

GUIDE TO SYMBOLS & ARROWS

To help you understand the techniques and the weblink we have used the following...

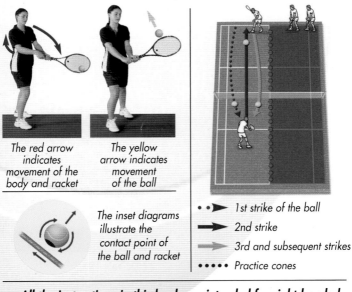

The red arrow indicates movement of the body and racket

The yellow arrow indicates movement of the ball

The inset diagrams illustrate the contact point of the ball and racket

• • ► 1st strike of the ball

► 2nd strike

► 3rd and subsequent strikes

• • • • • Practice cones

All the instructions in this book are intended for right-handed players. Left-handed players should simply reverse the instructions.

Log on to www.activology.com where you see this sign to view live-action clips.

THE COURT

When you are learning the game you can practise your skills by hitting a ball against a wall or playing rallies with friends where there is a flat, hard surface, but to play a proper match you will need a tennis court.

WHITE LINES

The markings on a tennis court are always white and indicate the extremities of the court and service courts. The ball is counted as 'in' if any part of the ball lands on the line, and 'out' if it lands on the other side of it.

THE BASELINE

The baseline marks each end of the court, and the ball must land on or inside this line, when hit from the opposite side of the net. Players must also have both feet behind this line when serving. It is 10.97 metres (36 ft) wide.

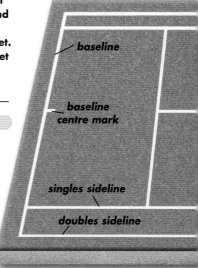

baseline

baseline centre mark

singles sideline

doubles sideline

BASELINE CENTRE MARK

This marks the centre of the baseline. Players serving on the right of this mark (looking up the court) must serve diagonally into the left-hand service box on the other side of the net, and vice versa. To start serving in a game you must serve from the right-hand side of the court.

SINGLE SIDELINES

The single sidelines mark the outer edge of the court for a singles match. They are 11.89 metres (39 ft) long either side of the net and 23.77 metres (78 ft) along the length of the whole court.

DOUBLE SIDELINES

These indicate the edge of the court for a doubles match. The double sidelines are 1.37 metres (4.5 ft) wide of the single sidelines. Together, these are known as the tramlines.

SURFACE

A tennis court can be a variety of surfaces, such as clay, grass, concrete, polished wood or even types of rubber or plastic. Rough surfaces, such as clay slow the ball down but make it bounce higher. Fast surfaces, such as grass make the ball skid and stay low as it bounces.

THE NET

The net is suspended from two posts that are 1.07 metres (3 ft 6 ins) high and overlap the court by 0.91 metres (3 ft) each side. The centre of the net measures 0.91 metres (3 ft).

SERVICE LINE

The service line is at 90 degrees to the centre service line. A ball landing between this line, the centre service line and the net (the service box) is counted as 'in'.

the net

service line

centre service line

service box

CENTRE SERVICE LINE

The centre service line divides the area between the net and the service line into two service boxes.

SERVICE BOX

The service box is the legal area into which the ball is served. There are two service boxes on each side of the court, measuring 6.4 metres (21 ft) in length and 4.12 metres (13.5 ft) in width. The server stands to one side of the baseline centre mark and serves the ball into the service box diagonally opposite. Service alternates between the two sides of the court after each point is scored.

EQUIPMENT

n ew and cheaper materials mean that there is a larger range of tennis equipment on the market than there used to be. Choose durable items that will feel comfortable to wear or a pleasure to use.

SHIRT

A tennis shirt must be loose enough to be comfortable but not too big that it impairs movement. It should be made of a soft, natural material like cotton to absorb sweat, and should feature small air-holes to give ventilation during play.

SKIRT

Women generally wear shorts, but tennis skirts and dresses are also available. They should be short enough to allow complete freedom of movement. Stretch fabrics are good as they are light and strong.

SOCKS

The best socks are made of cotton or towelling to absorb sweat and are thick on the foot area to prevent blisters.

BALLS

Tennis balls are 6.35–6.67 cm (2½–2 ⅝ inches) in diameter and made from two sections of rubber that are fused together and then covered in a tough fibrous combination of wool and synthetic material. The most common colour for tennis balls is fluorescent yellow.

RACKET

There are many kinds of racket made to suit different standards and styles of play. To choose a good racket, find one that feels comfortable. It should feel right in your hand and be light enough to swing but heavy enough to put some power into your shots.

head   racket face

throat

handle

butt

If you are a beginner, choose a light racket with a large head. This will be good for increasing the power of your shots. Basically, the larger the head, the bigger the area for hitting the ball – this is known as the 'sweet spot'. If you already have a good technique and can hit powerful shots, choose a stiffer, heavier racket; this will give you more control.

SHORTS

Tennis shorts should be loose and comfortable, but strong enough to survive the odd tumble. Pockets are useful for storing a second ball when serving.

FOOTWEAR

The right shoes are extremely important. They must be light and comfortable, with the leather and synthetic upper part offering flexibility as well as support for the foot, ankle and toes. Non-marking soles are a must if you want to play on a tennis court. Tennis shoes are very different to cross trainers or running shoes. Rubber soles are designed to give maximum grip on the court.

BODY POSITION

One of the most crucial lessons to learn in tennis is how best to position your body to play a shot. With good footwork you can prepare for your shot as soon as the ball is played to you, getting into position early so that you can react to your opponent's shot. If you wait until the ball is right in front of you it will be too late.

READY POSITION

The ready position is the stance adopted between shots. It gives maximum flexibility and balance to return a shot.

SPLIT-STEP POSITION

The split-step is a small bounce you make just before moving to the ball. The timing of it is crucial. You must try to make your bounce just before your opponent strikes the ball. This makes you alert and ready to move in any direction.

STEP 1 After the split-step, turn in the direction of the ball coming towards you. Take the racket back and move to the ball, in this case with a forehand stroke (see pages 16–17).

STEP 2

As you approach the ball, assess your distance from it in order to hit it comfortably. This is called the 'contact point', where the ball must be in front of your body but not too close. Hit the ball in the direction you want it to go.

STEP 3

Get back into the ready position to prepare for the next shot.

PLAYING TO WIN

Being a good tennis player is about mastering several skills at once. You need to:

- be alert to anticipate the movement of the ball and reach it in time for a good return.
- always focus on the ball.
- stay balanced with a low centre of gravity.
- use the split-step to reach the ball quickly.
- try to assess the angle of your racket and the direction of the ball in order to play the best return shot.
- adjust the power of your swing to return the most appropriate shot.

GRIPS

the way you hold your tennis racket is called your grip. There are a variety of recognised grips, all of which are correct, but some are more effective in certain situations or when playing a particular shot. The most important thing is that your grip feels comfortable and that you are able to hit the ball cleanly.

RIGHT-HANDED OR LEFT-HANDED?

All the grips shown here are for right-handed players. If you are left-handed, simply do the reverse.

FINDING YOUR GRIP

Use the 'V' to help you find the correct grip

Hold your racket in your right hand, as if you are shaking hands with it. Look at the 'V' between your thumb and first finger (see above). Make sure this is at the top of the handle.

Look at the base of your racket's handle. You will see that it has eight sides. The 'V' between your thumb and first finger moves around the handle depending on the grip.

FOREHAND GRIPS

There are four main forehand grips, used for playing balls that are approaching you on your racket side.

EASTERN

This is a nice, natural-feeling grip, suitable for beginners. Simply hold the racket with the 'V' of your hand on edge 2.

CONTINENTAL

This is a more advanced grip, which many players use for serving. The 'V' should be on edge 1. The continental grip gives more power on certain shots and aids flexibility in the wrist, offering greater variation .

WESTERN

The western grip originated with the introduction of courts, which produce high-bouncing balls. The 'V' is positioned on edge 4. This will feel awkward as your wrist is wrapped right around the handle.

SEMI-WESTERN

The semi-western grip is a toned-down version of the western, also used for hitting high balls. The 'V' is positioned on edge 3.

When a ball is approaching you on your left side, you will
need to hit a backhand stroke. To do this, you can hold your
racket with one hand or two. Most beginners opt for the
double-handed version as it offers more control. However, use
whichever feels most natural.

ONE-HANDED BACKHAND

*The most common one-handed grip is the eastern
backhand. Rotate your wrist anti-clockwise around
the handle so your 'V' is on edge 8. To produce more
topspin (see page 17) position the 'V' on number 7.*

You can use two grips when doing a double-handed backhand.
The first is where you maintain an eastern forehand grip
with your right hand so your left arm gives you the power to
hit the ball. The second is where your right hand changes from
a forehand grip to a backhand grip, which gives more of the
power to your right arm (your left hand is simply supporting
the racket). See which one feels the most comfortable for you.

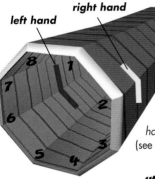

left hand   **right hand**

WITHOUT CHANGE

*Your right hand 'V' should
be on edge 2 and your left
hand should be on the handle,
above your right hand, with its
'V' on position 6 or 7, depending
on comfort. The closer your left
hand is to position 6, the more topspin
(see page 17) you will be able to exert.*

WITH CHANGE

*You should rotate your right hand anti-clockwise
round the handle so the 'V' is on edge 8, and your
left hand should be above it, with the 'V' on edge 7
or 6,(6 gives you more topspin).*

TOPSPIN SINGLE-HANDED

*This grips helps put topspin on the ball. Your right hand
'V' should be on edge 7, with your left hand supporting the
racket at the throat, until you release the racket to hit the ball.*

*After playing a shot, you should always come back to the ready position
with the racket in front of you. This is the point where you can change your
grip according to your opponent's shot, although you may find that you
only need to use one or two grips throughout the game.*

RULES OF PLAY

*t*ennis can be played as a 'singles' (one against one) or a 'doubles' match (two against two). The object of the game is to win points against your opponent/s. These points are accumulated to make 'games' and 'sets', and the winner is the first player to win two sets, in a three-set match, or three, in a five-set match.

SERVING

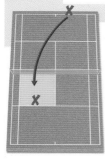

Having decided who serves first, the ball is played diagonally into the service box opposite. The server stands behind the baseline on the right-hand side. If the ball does not land in the service box, the umpire calls 'second service' and the player has another chance. If the second service is not successful then a 'double fault' is called and the opponent wins a point. If the ball hits the net cord but still lands inside the service box, then 'let' is called and the service can be taken again. This can happen on both first and second serves. After the first point is played, the server moves to the left-hand side of the baseline and serves diagonally into the other service box, alternating in this way for each point. If a ball that has been served strikes the opponent anywhere before it has bounced (even if it is going out) then the point goes to the server.

RECEIVING

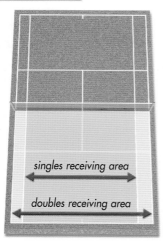

singles receiving area

doubles receiving area

If the server lands the ball in the service box, the opponent returns it over the net to continue play. It must land within the specified boundaries of the court. A rally is played with a point being scored for the last player to hit the ball over the net and in to the opposition's side of the court. If the ball hits the net cord as it goes over then play continues. The ball is only allowed to bounce once each time (unless you are in a wheelchair then it is allowed to bounce twice).

CHANGING ENDS

Once the first game is won, the players change ends and the service changes hands. Subsequently the players change ends every odd (1, 3, 5, 7, 9) game, but service changes hands at the end of every game.

SCORING

During a game, scoring goes in a set sequence. After the first point a player scores '15', followed by '30' and then '40'. If a player has no points then his score is 'love'. For example, if the server wins a point then the score is '15/love', as the server's score is always called first. To win a game a player must win four points before their opponent wins three. In the event of a tie break at '40' all, 'deuce' is called. After 'deuce', the score goes 'advantage X' (X being the player who wins the next point) and that player must win the following point to win the game. If he loses, the score returns to 'deuce'.

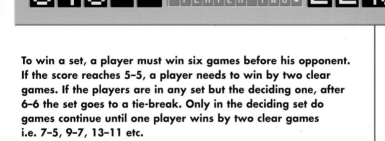

To win a set, a player must win six games before his opponent. If the score reaches 5–5, a player needs to win by two clear games. If the players are in any set but the deciding one, after 6–6 the set goes to a tie-break. Only in the deciding set do games continue until one player wins by two clear games i.e. 7–5, 9–7, 13–11 etc.

TIE-BREAK

The object of the tie-break is to be the first to score seven points. A server plays the first point, then the service changes after every two points. If the score reaches 6-6 the first player to gain a clear two-point advantage wins the set i.e. 8–6, 10–8, 12–10 etc.

DOUBLES

The rules for doubles matches are exactly the same, except that the doubles sidelines form the boundary of the court, with team players taking it in turns to serve and receive.

WARMING UP

as you pound up and down the court during a game of tennis you are working literally hundreds of muscles and tendons in your body. To protect them from injury and to maximise your flexibility, you should begin a match with a proper warm-up and stretching routine.

KNOCKING UP

Before a match you are allowed a five-minute 'knock-up' to get a feel for the ball. Players should knock the ball backwards and forwards, both taking the opportunity to come to the net for a minute or so to practise volleys and smashes. It is advisable to practise with a friend before a match to warm up properly.

FITNESS DRILLS

Because tennis is a high impact game, it helps to practise rapid, short bursts of movements. These drills improve speed and coordination.

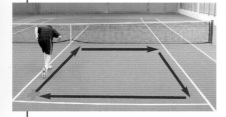

FOOTWORK SQUARE

Stand in the bottom corner of the service box. Run along the centre line to the net. At the net stop and sidestep along it to the sideline, then run backwards until you reach the service line. Finally, sidestep back to your starting position.

Stay facing the net at all times. Do the circuit five times and as fast as possible, taking a break between each one. The work/rest ratio should be 1:3.

PICK UP FITNESS

Crouch down behind the doubles sideline looking across the court, with four balls on the ground beside you. Pick up the first ball and place it on the first singles sideline ahead of you, then return, pick up another ball and run to the centre line to place it there. Return for the third ball and run to place it on the far singles sideline. Finally, collect the fourth ball and place it on the far doubles sideline. Go back to the starting point and repeat the drill in reverse order. Again, the work/rest ratio should be 1:3.

You can begin your warm-up with a gentle five-minute jog around the court – this will warm and loosen the muscles. Start stretching and take it gently. Never hold a stretch if it hurts – just take it to the point where you feel tension and hold for 10 or 15 seconds. Do not bounce when stretching.

ANKLE STRETCH

Lift each foot in turn so that only the toes are touching the ground, and gently turn your heel in both directions.

HAMSTRING STRETCH

Step forward with one leg and push the other out behind you to stretch the hamstring in the back of your leg. Repeat with the other leg.

PELICAN STRETCH

Stand on one leg and gather your foot in your hand. Gently pull it back behind you, stretching the pelican muscle at the front of your leg by easing your toes towards your buttock. Repeat with the other leg.

INNER THIGH STRETCH

With one leg bent, extend the other sideways until you can feel the tension in your groin. Hold the stretch for 15 seconds and repeat with the other leg.

WRIST & ARM STRETCH

Extend your arms out in front of you. Cup one hand into the other and push your thumbs against each other to stretch your arms and wrists.

FOREHAND STROKES

*t*he forehand drive is the shot you will probably feel most comfortable with and use the most. It is played when the ball is on your strongest side (your racket side), giving you more control of the ball. The forehand drive can be aimed deep or wide into the opposing court. This makes it harder to return, putting your opponent under pressure and hopefully stopping them from playing an attacking shot against you.

FOREHAND DRIVE

The forehand drive is a groundstroke, which means the ball is played after it has bounced.

STEP 1 From the split-step position, pivot your feet to the right to turn the shoulder. Begin to take the racket back.

STEP 2 Focusing on the ball at all times, bring your racket right back behind your shoulder and stretch your non-racket hand out for balance in the direction you want the ball to go.

STEP 3 Step forward and swing the racket smoothly but firmly into contact with the ball.

STEP 4 Follow through with your racket reaching the opposite shoulder. Your body has now rotated naturally so that you are facing down the court. Notice how your weight has transferred to your front foot, with the back heel now off the ground.

TOPSPIN

Topspin is the name for the spin you put on the ball when you hit it in a certain way. Brush up underneath the ball instead of hitting it though the middle. When you hit the ball with topspin, it rises higher over the net, and comes up higher than normal when it bounces, confusing your opponent. This is a difficult technique to master, but worth the practice.

Bend your knees so that your body is low. As you make contact with the ball, brush your racket upwards on it, causing it to spin as you hit it. Your body should rise up with the ball.

OPEN-STANCE FOREHAND DRIVE

The open-stance forehand drive is used to deal with higher bouncing balls. It can be used with all forehand grips.

STEP 1 *Step across to the ball and bring your racket back.*

STEP 2 *Transfer your weight to your leading leg, twisting your shoulders round. Reach around the outside of the ball when hitting to give it some spin.*

TOP TIP

Use the forearm to roll the racket around the ball a bit like a windscreen wiper action. This gives the ball more spin to stop it from going out of the court.

BACKHAND STROKES

i f the ball comes to you on your non-racket side you will
have to bring your racket across your body and hit the
ball with the reverse side. This shot is called a backhand,
and can be played with either one hand or two.

DOUBLE-HANDED BACKHAND DRIVE

**Approximately half of all players use a double-
handed backhand drive to give them more power
and control than the single-handed version.**

STEP 1 *From the split-step position,
turn and pivot your feet to the left. Bring your
racket back and twist your body round so
that your shoulder is square on to the ball.*

STEP 2 *Bring your front foot
forward so that you are side-on
to the ball approaching you.*

STEP 4
*Continue to follow
through with your
racket, turning
your shoulders
and bringing
your back foot
round so that
you are facing
the net. You are
now ready for the
next shot.*

STEP 3 *In one fluid
movement, swing the
racket towards the ball.
Your body should follow
through naturally. Keep
your arms loose and your
grip firm as you bring
the racket round to make
contact with the ball,
just in front of your body.*

TOP TIP

*Try to vary your spins to keep
your opponent guessing.*

SINGLE-HANDED BACKHAND DRIVE

The single-handed backhand drive is used to reach wider shots, although it may not give you the power of the double-handed backhand drive when learning.

STEP 1 From the split-step position, turn and pivot to the left, so that your front shoulder is square-on to the ball. At the same time bring your racket back across your chest, using your non-hitting hand to grip the throat of the racket.

STEP 2 Step forward into the ball with your leading foot, bending your knees and crouching down slightly as you prepare to make your swing.

STEP 3 Release the racket from your non-hitting hand and smoothly swing it towards the ball. Keep side-on to the ball as you make contact with it in front of your body.

STEP 4 Follow through with your racket, keeping your elbow straight with your racket facing skywards.

SLICED BACKHAND

STEP 1 Using a continental grip, position yourself slightly wide of the ball and open up the racket face.

The sliced backhand keeps the ball low by putting backspin on it.

STEP 2 Slice the ball from high to low, and follow through with the racket parallel to your body. The ball bounces low to outmanoeuvre your opponent.

ON THE COURT: GROUNDSTROKES

g roundstrokes are those where the ball bounces once before it is struck. Most commonly, these are the forehand and backhand strokes. These drills are designed not just to help you practise getting the ball back over the net, but to get it into the areas of the court that your opponent would find difficult to reach.

THROWN BALL DRILL

This develops control and accuracy of the ball.

Pairs of players stand opposite each other in one half of a court. Player A, from each pair, throws a ball underarm so that it bounces in front of his partner, Player B who is standing on the baseline. Player B plays a controlled forehand back for Player A to catch. After 10 hits, the drill is repeated to the backhand.

PROGRESSION

The feeders move to the other side of the net. Using a racket, they hit the ball to the receivers who have to play the groundstroke over the net. After each drill, the feeder gradually moves back until they play the final drill on the opposite baseline.

TARGET SHOOTING

Target shooting improves accuracy to the areas of the court that are difficult to reach.

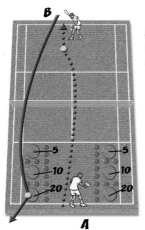

One half of a court is marked out with coloured cones indicating three target areas (see diagram). Player A feeds either a forehand or a backhand to Player B on the opposite baseline. Player B must play a groundstroke, aiming to land it in one of the target areas (scoring either 5, 10 or 20 points). Five points are deducted for every shot, that lands outside either of the target areas. After 25 shots the players swap roles. The winner is the one with the most points.

OUT OF BOUNDS

This develops accuracy in a rally situation.

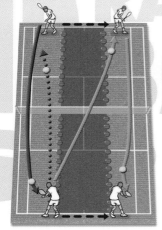

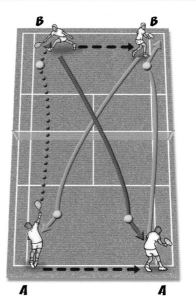

A court is divided into three sections with cones (see diagram). Two players must then play a rally in which the central section is 'out of bounds'. The players should attempt to keep the ball in play within the legal areas.

DOWN THE LINE V CROSS-COURT

This requires quick reactions and speed to keep the ball in play.

Player A feeds a ball underarm down the sideline to Player B's forehand. Player B returns it, cross-court, to Player A's opposite corner. Player A runs across the court to play the ball down the line to Player B's backhand. Player B returns the ball, cross-court, to where the drill began. After five minutes the players swap roles.

THE SERVICE

The service is probably the most important shot in tennis. It is also one of the most difficult. A fast serve close to the centre or sidelines of the service box will be difficult for your opponent to return, giving you the advantage.

SERVING

▲ Try to think of the service as one continuous, fluid movement. When you start, don't try to hit the ball too hard, but concentrate on a smooth, direct stroke.

HOLDING THE BALL

As you prepare to toss the ball, hold it lightly. The momentum of the ball will come from the upward swing of your arm, so you should simply release it. Try not to flick it with your fingers.

STEP 1 Get your feet into position behind the baseline, side-on to the net. When you are balanced and ready, hold your racket out in front of you with the ball at the throat or against the strings.

STEP 2 Bring your hands down together and shift your weight from your front foot to your back foot making sure that you focus on the ball.

STEP 3 Now bring your arms up together. As you throw the ball up into the air, slightly in front of you, your racket should move back into position ready to hit the ball at the same time.

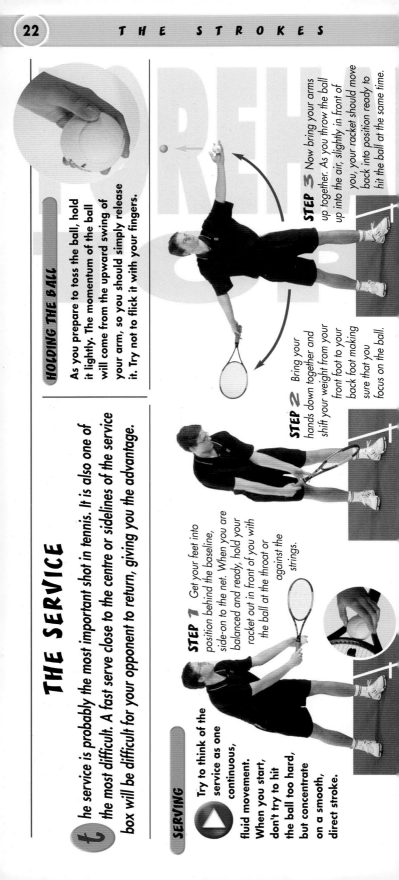

FOOT FAULT

Although you are allowed to jump into the court as you serve, your feet must not touch the ground inside the court or the baseline until the ball has been struck. If this happens it is called a 'foot fault', and it will disqualify your serve.

STEP 4 Watch the ball as it rises, bending your knees and shifting your weight onto your front foot. Bend your hitting arm so that you bring your racket back behind your head. Notice the arms form the shape of a tick.

STEP 5 As the ball reaches its highest point, straighten your legs and push onto your toes. Stretch your arm for balance and drop the racket behind your shoulder, keeping your elbow up.

STEP 6 As you extend your racket arm, your shoulders rotate so that your chest faces the net as you make contact with the ball. Hit the ball at the highest point you can reach. Bring your non-hitting arm back into your body as your racket arm goes forward.

STEP 7 Keeping your head up, follow the ball through, allowing your forward momentum to continue. Return to the ready position.

Do not serve until you are ready. Bounce the ball a little to focus your mind and take a deep breath to relax yourself before serving. If anything distracts your concentration, stop and start again.

ON THE COURT: THE SERVICE

y ou get two chances to get the ball into the service area. However, it is good practice to aim to get it in on the first attempt. The failure of the first serve may give your opponent a chance to attack a slower second serve.

THROWING DRILL

Place a racket on the ground in front of your feet, pointing ahead of you. Then go through the motions of serving. Throw the ball so that it lands on the racket face every time. This will really improve your ball toss.

CONSECUTIVE SERVING

Gaining practice on the serve will ensure more accurate service during a game.

One player serves to the other. If successful, he moves to the other side of the court to serve again. There are no second serves in this drill, so as soon as one player misses the other takes over. Aim to serve 10 consecutive, successful serves.

SERVING FOR DEPTH

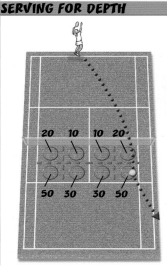

This will enable you to practise and improve hitting deep serves.

Divide the service areas on one side of a court in half widthways (see diagram). Two players serve two balls in a row, taking it in turns. The players score points according to where their serves land. After five minutes, the player with the most points wins.

20 10 10 20

50 30 30 50

TARGET SERVING

Once you have mastered getting the ball into the service area, you can try this drill to hit specific areas of the service box.

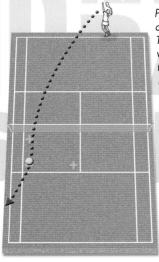

Place cones on the corners of one service box (see diagram). These are the three areas from where a service is the hardest to return. A successful serve that is not returned is called an 'ace'. The aim of the drill is to hit the cones and knock them over. Players have 30 balls each and score 10 points every time they hit a marker. The winner is the player with the most points.

ONE-SERVE MATCH

This drill should improve first-service success in match situations.

Two players play a match, but with no second services allowed. This makes achieving a successful first serve even more crucial to the match than usual and gets players used to serving in pressure situations – for instance on break point.

SERVICE RETURNS

t he kind of service return you play depends on the kind of serve you receive. Service returns account for 50 per cent of the game and it is important to practise them as much as the serve. You will be a stronger player if your shots are difficult to return.

RETURNING THE BALL

Returning a serve is all about seeing the ball early and reacting to it quickly. Stand back from the baseline as it is better to come towards a ball than to run backwards.

STEP 1 Stand in the ready position roughly 0.3 metres (1 ft) back from where you expect to hit the ball.

STEP 2 As your opponent tosses the ball, take a step forward.

STEP 3 Split-step (see page 8) as your opponent strikes the ball.

STEP 4 As the ball leaves your opponent's racket, judge its flight and adjust your position to give yourself room. Turn to the side on which the ball is coming and take your racket back, in this case, using a forehand stroke.

STEP 5 As the ball comes towards you, step forward and bring your racket onto it, making contact just in front of your body. Follow through with the racket and the power of your arm stroke. Keep your wrists firm and use your non-hitting arm for balance.

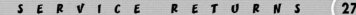

BLOCKED FOREHAND

When the serve is very powerful, the best return is often a blocked forehand return. The skill here is to hold the racket firmly and angle it to punch the ball back over the net. The action is similar to a volley *(see pages 30–31)*.

BACKHAND RETURN

STEP 1
From the split-step position, turn your body to the backhand side, judging how much take-back you will need from the power of the serve.

STEP 2 *Step forward to the ball. Watch it make contact with the racket as you keep your wrists firmly locked. Follow through to complete the return.*

SINGLE-HANDED BACKHAND RETURN

The same footwork rules apply to the single-handed backhand return. However, because you have a longer reach than with a double-handed return, this is an extremely useful return for reaching wide, sliced serves curving away from you.

Concentrate on where you are going to aim the ball. A high return without pace in the centre of the court is easy for your opponent to volley away for a winning shot or groundstroke. Move your feet into position to hit the best shot possible.

ON THE COURT: SERVICE RETURNS

*O*nce you have the basic grasp of the groundstrokes, you can concentrate on adding power and direction to your return. Experiment with the grips to see which ones give you more control on certain serves.

BASIC RETURNS

Start with easy shots to build up your service return confidence.

Player A stands just behind the baseline of the court while Player B hits a medium-pace serve over the net and into the service box for Player A to return. Practise for 10 minutes and then swap places with the server.

PROGRESSION

Once both players are hitting the ball cleanly and getting it back over the net every time, start trying to place your shots close to the sidelines and the baseline.

FAST RETURNS

Returning a hard and fast serve is all about reading the serve and getting into position to attack it.

Player A stands just behind the baseline, while Player B serves from the service line on the other side of the net. However, this time Player B plays a full-pace serve into the service box. Player A must attempt to return these hard and fast serves.

ATTACKING RETURNS

Use this drill to practise playing accurate and aggressive service returns.

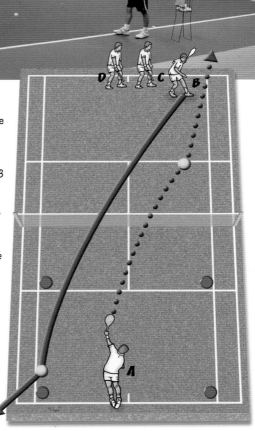

Place cones at one end of the court (see diagram). Player A stands at the same end as the markers and serves. Player B must try to hit one of the markers with his return. Every hit scores 10 points. After five minutes, Player B goes to the back of the queue. Player C repeats the drill, followed by Player D.

The cones represent the perfect points to aim for when hitting a return of serve. Your opponent will have to run to get the ball, giving him less time to make a successful return.

TOP TIP
Take smaller backswings to block big, fast serves.

THE VOLLEY

a volley is a shot played before the ball has bounced, usually from an attacking position close to the net. When you play a volley you are simply re-directing the ball, using the angle of the racket head to send the ball back over the net.

FOREHAND VOLLEY

▲ You can volley a ball using any of the forehand grips, however, a continental grip is good for reaching the angle of a low volley.

STEP 1

Get yourself into position about 1.5 metres (5 ft) from the net and stand in the ready position. Split-step as the ball is played and prepare to receive the shot.

STEP 2

After you have landed, with the ball coming towards you, turn and pivot your feet in the direction of the approaching ball. Keep your racket ahead of you as you angle it in the direction of the ball. Take it back very slightly.

STEP 3

Step forward with the foot on your non-racket side, shifting your weight onto the front foot as you position your racket to meet the ball. Angle the racket to direct the ball towards one of the sidelines or away from your opponent. Do not follow through after impact.

HIGH BACKHAND VOLLEY

This stroke requires good timing. Play it sideways, stretch out your free arm for balance and squeeze the grip as you make contact with the ball. You can use your other hand for extra support or put your thumb up the back of the grip.

LOW BACKHAND VOLLEY

Approach the ball side-on and step forward with the front foot on your racket-side. Bend your knees and go down to hit the ball. Hold your body position and freeze your racket for a split-second. This will give you the right amount of power to make the volley. Keep the racket head above the wrist.

HIGH FOREHAND VOLLEY

To reach a high ball, bring your shoulders round slightly so that you can reach up and over the ball to punch it down. Hold the racket after you have made contact to avoid sweeping the ball down into the net.

LOW FOREHAND VOLLEY

Lunge forward with the front foot on your non-racket side and bend your knees to get your body low. Keep your head up and open your racket face to get it under the ball. The momentum from the ball will lift it back over the net. Keep your back as straight as you can, keeping the racket head above the wrist at all times.

BACKHAND VOLLEY

The backhand volley is played from a more side-on position than the forehand. This more natural posture makes it an easier shot to play. The continental grip is the strongest, but a backhand or double-handed grip will work well.

STEP 1
As the ball approaches your backhand side, turn your body sideways, bringing your racket back.

STEP 2 Step forward to meet the ball, then bring the racket under the ball to angle it back over the net. Keep the wrists locked and the racket up. Following through slightly after impact will give more punch to the stroke.

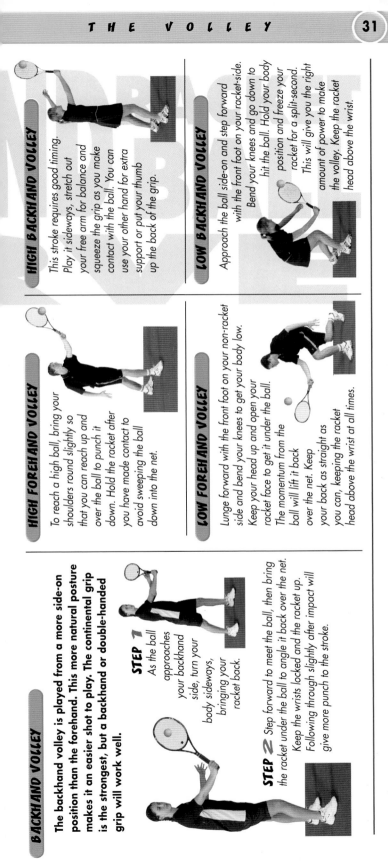

ON THE COURT: THE VOLLEY

h itting a controlled volley takes plenty of practise, and these drills are designed to slowly build up your skills at the net. A lethal weapon in the tennis player's armoury, a well-hit volley is almost impossible to return.

THE 'NO RACKET' VOLLEY

This teaches you the basic footwork and body position required to hit a good volley.

Two players, without rackets, stand opposite each other, about 4 metres (12 ft) apart. Player A throws a ball in the air to player B's forehand side. Player B must step forward with the opposite foot and catch the ball just in front of him with his racket hand. Player B then repeats the exercise for Player A. After practising the forehand side the players should switch to a backhand catch.

VOLLEY DEVELOPMENT

This drill slowly builds you up to hitting technically correct volleys.

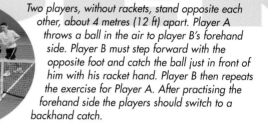

STEP 1

Two players stand on opposite sides of the net, 4 metres (12 ft) apart. Player A throws the ball to Player B's forehand side. Player B, holding the racket at the throat, must volley it back. This is much easier than hitting a volley holding the racket by its handle.

STEP 2

Standing in the same position, Player A throws the ball for Player B to volley it gently back, this time holding the racket in the normal position.

STEP 3

Finally, Players A and B both use their rackets and volley the ball between each other.

VOLLEY PAIRS

The previous drills concentrate on volleying on the spot. Use this drill to volley while on the move.

Players get into pairs and line up to one side of the net. The first pair begin volleying the ball to each other, while at the same time moving across the court, parallel to the net. They are followed by the second, and then the third pair. Each pair must try not to let the ball bounce or hit the net until they reach the other side. Repeat the drill using a variety of forehand and backhand volleys.

AT THE NET

Use this drill to practise defensive volleying at the net against hard, attempted passing shots.

Using marker cones, the court is split down the middle on both sides of the net (see diagram). Using only one half of the court. Player A starts from the service line and feeds underarm passes to Player B on the baseline. Both players then play out the point, with Player A on the service line and Player B on the baseline. Player A must try to volley on every shot. After the rally Player B goes to the back of the queue and Player C repeats the drill, followed by Player D.

TOP TIP

To make it harder for Player A, remove the cones on his side of the net. He now has a larger area to cover when returning the shot.

THE LOB

t he lob is a shot played high into the air and over an opponent who has come towards the net. It is an excellent stroke as it can force an opponent to play the return from a difficult angle, weakening their position in a rally.

FOREHAND LOB

It is important to hit this ball correctly. Too hard and it will go out of bounds, but too soft and you will present an easy smash *(see pages 38–39)* to your opponent. This stroke is often performed with an open racket, but a closed one will give the ball topspin and make it harder to return.

STEP 1 As the ball bounces, keep your legs apart and bend your knees as you get your racket back early.

STEP 2 After the ball has reached the top of its bounce, rotate your shoulders back and bring your racket round underneath it. Now lift the ball into the air.

STEP 3 Straighten your legs as you follow through, making sure that you don't under-hit the ball. Aim to lift the ball over your opponent's racket, while keeping it within the bounds of the court.

SINGLE-HANDED BACKHAND LOB

Power from the lob is played from the shoulder. You can play this shot with either an open racket face or a closed racket face for more topspin. It is a more attacking shot if played with topspin.

STEP 1 *Turn sideways-on to the ball and bend your knees as you take your racket back to a point below where you will hit the ball.*

STEP 2 *When the ball begins to fall after it has bounced, sweep your racket underneath to hit it.*

STEP 3 *Use your non-racket arm for balance as you straighten your legs. Rotate your shoulders back towards the net and follow through with the shot.*

DOUBLE-HANDED BACKHAND LOB

If you can put topspin on the ball when you lob it, you can give it more height and it will bounce sharply away from your opponent. In this case, your non-racket hand gives you more control.

STEP 1
Turn your shoulders back and drop the racket below the wrist.

STEP 2
With a slighty closed racket face, wait for the ball to bounce. As it begins to fall, sharply bring your racket up so that it sweeps up the back of the ball to exert topspin.

STEP 3
Your shoulders turn towards the net as you follow through. Straighten your legs and rotate your back leg up onto your toes.

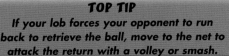

TOP TIP
If your lob forces your opponent to run back to retrieve the ball, move to the net to attack the return with a volley or smash.

ON THE COURT: THE LOB

t he lob is one of the hardest strokes to master as it requires the player to hit the ball high into the air, without it landing outside the court. These drills enable you to perfect the action of sweeping the ball up above your opponent's head to land in the court.

DEEP LOBBING

Use this drill to practise hitting lobs as far back into your opponent's court as possible.

Player A stands on the service line and feeds balls to Player B on the opposite baseline. Immediately after the feed, Player A raises the racket above her head. Player B must return the ball by lobbing it over Player A to land in the back section of the court.

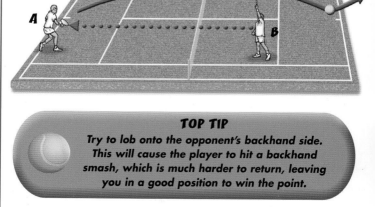

TOP TIP

Try to lob onto the opponent's backhand side. This will cause the player to hit a backhand smash, which is much harder to return, leaving you in a good position to win the point.

TARGET LOBBING

As the lob is a difficult shot you can use this drill to help you gain better control and direction when you need it most.

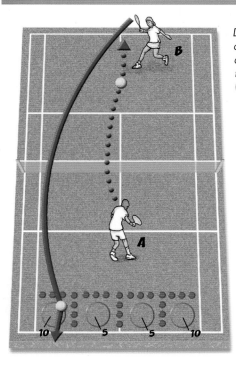

Divide the end of a court into four boxes and allocate points for each section (see diagram). Player A stands in the centre of the service line and feeds balls to Player B at the opposite baseline. Player B must lob the balls back over Player A's head, aiming for the scoring boxes. Add the points up each time the ball lands in one of the boxes. After 20 shots the players swap roles. The winner is the one with the most points.

B

A

10   5   5   10

THE SMASH

he smash is an attacking shot, played when the ball is in the air above your head. You will need to play it with confidence, otherwise it may be returned with a shot that will force you to run backwards to reach it. This could weaken your position in the rally and give your opponent a greater chance of securing the point.

FOREHAND SMASH

You can use an eastern grip to get instant results when you are learning, but try to change to a continental grip as you gain confidence. This will give the shot more power and spin.

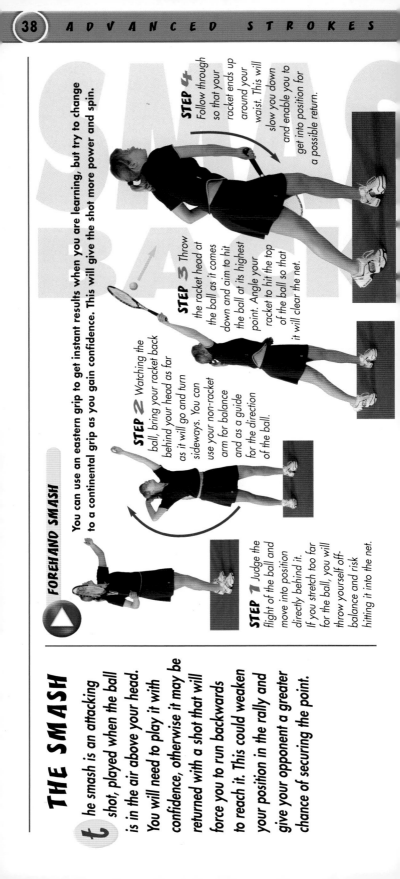

STEP 1 Judge the flight of the ball and move into position directly behind it. If you stretch too far for the ball, you will throw yourself off-balance and risk hitting it into the net.

STEP 2 Watching the ball, bring your racket back behind your head as far as it will go and turn sideways. You can use your non-racket arm for balance and as a guide for the direction of the ball.

STEP 3 Throw the racket head at the ball as it comes down and aim to hit the ball at its highest point. Angle your racket to hit the top of the ball so that it will clear the net.

STEP 4 Follow through so that your racket ends up around your waist. This will slow you down and enable you to get into position for a possible return.

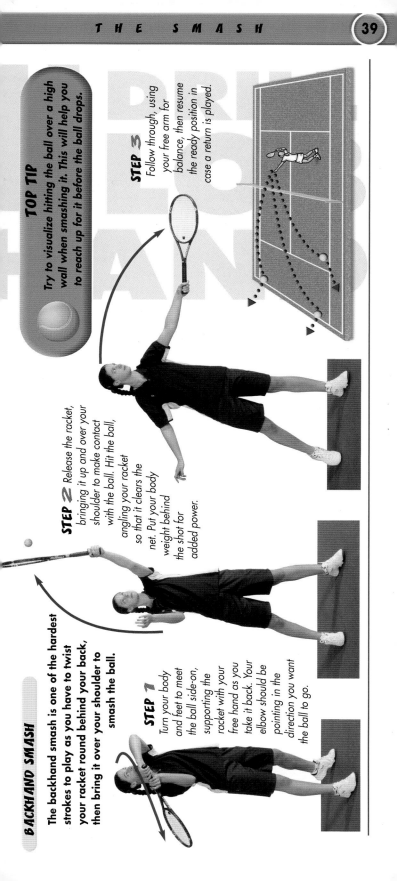

TOP TIP

Try to visualize hitting the ball over a high wall when smashing it. This will help you to reach up for it before the ball drops.

STEP 3
Follow through, using your free arm for balance, then resume the ready position in case a return is played.

STEP 2 Release the racket, bringing it up and over your shoulder to make contact with the ball. Hit the ball, angling your racket so that it clears the net. Put your body weight behind the shot for added power.

BACKHAND SMASH

The backhand smash is one of the hardest strokes to play as you have to twist your racket round behind your back, then bring it over your shoulder to smash the ball.

STEP 1
Turn your body and feet to meet the ball side-on, supporting the racket with your free hand as you take it back. Your elbow should be pointing in the direction you want the ball to go.

ON THE COURT: THE SMASH

When you get a chance to smash in a match, it is important to kill the point there and then. If the shot is returned, use your whole body to get maximum power behind it, making it as hard as possible to return a second time.

THE 'NO HIT' SMASH

The smash requires excellent balance and footwork so use this drill to anticipate the movement of the ball during play.

Two players stand opposite each other on either side of the net. Player A throws the ball into the air above Player B's head. Player B gets into position, sideways on, with his racket back and non-hitting arm fully extended above him. As the ball comes over, he should catch it to become familiar with the flight of the ball.

SMASH TO OPEN COURT

Build up confidence in your stroke using this simple drill.

Player A stands at one end of the baseline and feeds a ball with an open racket to Player B who is standing in midcourt. Player B must smash the ball back into the open court. To add a competitive edge, each player has 20 smash attempts, scoring one point for every winning shot and five for hitting a line.

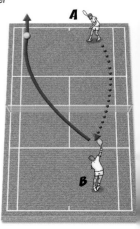

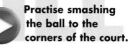

Practise smashing the ball to the corners of the court.

Using cones, mark out four boxes at one end of the court (see diagram). Player A stands at this end of the court, lobbing balls to player B on the other side of the net. Player B smashes the ball back, aiming for the target boxes. After 20 shots, the players swap roles. The winner is the one with the most points.

PROGRESSION

In a match, you are normally running back when you hit a smash because your opponent is attempting to lob you. To re-create this situation, Player B should run forward and touch the net between each shot.

THE DROP SHOT

a drop shot is where you hit the ball so that it drops over the net with a soft bounce. It can be used to draw a player out of position, by forcing him to come into the net, or to win a point when you have already forced your opponent to the back of the court with a previous return.

FOREHAND DROP SHOT

You can play the drop shot when you are close to the net, using your preferred forehand grip. The eastern grip is used in this demonstration.

STEP 1 As the ball reaches you, take your racket back farther than you would for a volley. Step forwards onto your non-racket foot.

STEP 2 As the ball approaches you, try to slice the ball on the rise with a slight downward motion of the racket. Reduce your follow-through as if playing a volley. This shot is performed by applying a firm grip but having 'soft hands'.

TOP TIP

By taking your racket back early, as you would for a normal groundstroke, you can disguise the drop shot.

BACKHAND DROP SHOT

This can be played with one or two hands, using your preferred backhand grip.

STEP 1 *Get side-on to the ball and pull your racket back.*

STEP 2 *As you step forwards, reduce your swing, slicing the back of the ball as it rises. Keep your follow-through short. This shot should be played with a slightly open racket face at contact point.*

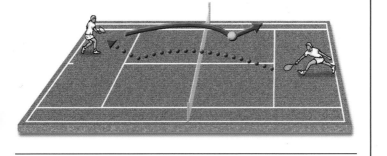

DROP VOLLEY

This is a drop shot that is played before the ball has touched the ground.

Approach this shot in the same way you would approach a normal volley, but angle your racket more. As you make contact, loosen your grip so that the racket head moves back slightly and the strings absorb the pace of the ball. It should just drop neatly over the net. You can use a forehand or backhand stroke depending on the direction of the ball.

DIET

y ou can give yourself more energy and stamina on the court by eating and drinking the right foods both before and during the game. A healthy diet and regular exercise will benefit anyone, but for sportsmen and women this is essential to become a top athelete.

BASIC DIET

This food chart gives you the basic principles of a balanced diet, ideal for athletes.

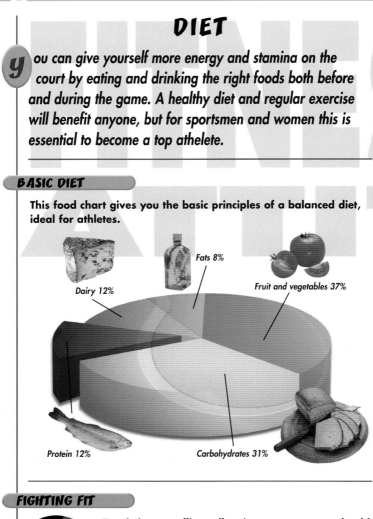

Fats 8%

Dairy 12%

Fruit and vegetables 37%

Protein 12%

Carbohydrates 31%

FIGHTING FIT

Tennis is a gruelling, all-action game, so you should tailor your food according to your match schedule and try not to eat too much before a game.

A light, balanced meal, one to one and half hours before a match is ideal. A tennis match can last anything from one to four hours, so it is important to replenish your fluids before, during and after a match. Water is the best drink, although the body needs some sugars, so you can add a small amount of cordial or fruit juice. It is very important to stay hydrated at all times.

ENERGY BUSTERS

Carry fast-digesting snacks, such as bananas or fruit snack bars to keep your energy levels up – especially if the game is a long one.

Do not eat sugary foods as this will give you a high burst of energy and then leave you feeling empty.

MENTAL ATTITUDE

a s well as preparing the body, it is also important to prepare the mind for a tennis match. At the end of the day, much of your ability as a player comes from self-confidence and self-belief.

VISUALISE SUCCESS

During a game, take some time alone to focus your mind on the task ahead.

Use positive thinking and concentration to visualise yourself winning the next point and in turn the set and match. If things are going badly or a decision goes against you, then you must learn not to get upset or lose confidence.

MIND OVER MATTER

There is nothing like winning a game to give you confidence.

An outward display of euphoria, at times like this, will put pressure on your opponent. In tennis, winning is as much a battle of wills as of technical skill.

FIT FOR THE TOP

All professional tennis players do other activities to enhance their performance.

Golf is perhaps the most preferred sport for tennis players as it allows them to relax without risk of injury.

HOW THE FAMOUS DO IT

m ost people play tennis for fun, but the very best players in the world are professionals who travel the world playing the game AND get paid for it. However, don't think it's all glamour in the world of a tennis pro; it takes hard work and dedication to make it to the top... and even more to stay there.

LIFE ON TOUR

Professional tennis is played by men on the ATP Tour (the Association of Tennis Professionals) and by women on the WTA Tour (the Women's Tennis Association).

The top four grand slam events are the Australian Open, the French Open, Wimbledon and the U.S. Open. Events occur from Austria to Saudi Arabia – this means that for most players it's a case of stepping on and off a plane as they compete to pick up crucial world ranking points. Gustavo Keurten, seen here at the French Open in 1997, is a top ranking player.

TYPICAL MATCH DAY

8.00	Wake up
8.30	Eat a low fat, high enegy breakfast with no fried foods
9.00	Arrive at the event venue

9.15	Warm up/stretch
9.30	Practice on court with a coach or another pro
11.30	Eat a light lunch
12.00	Discuss pre-match tactics with the coach
12.30	Rest and stretch/change into kit
2.00	Play a match
4.0	Attend a post-match press conference
4.30	Do a light gym workout/stretch
6.00	Swim/rub down
7.00	Return to the hotel
8.00	Eat a high carbohydrate dinner
9.00	Watch a video of the match with the coach
10.30	Go to bed

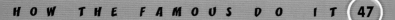
PRIZE MONEY

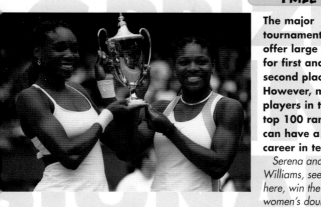

The major tournaments offer large prizes for first and second place. However, many players in the top 100 ranking can have a great career in tennis.

Serena and Venus Williams, seen here, win the women's doubles final at Wimbledon in 2000. Prize money varies with each tournament but the winner of the mens singles final can receive in excess of £400,000.

THE PRESS & MULTIMEDIA

Doing press, TV and radio interviews is all part of the daily routine for successful tennis players.

Win or lose, after a match they will be expected to attend a press conference to talk about the game. On top of that they will be asked to do exclusive interviews and photo shoots with

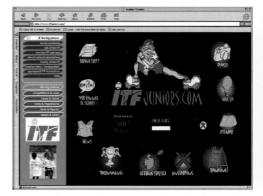

TV stations and publications. Many players and associations have their own websites that are updated regularly – particularly during a major tournament.

MONEY

For the top players the rewards in tennis can be enormous.

Stars like Andre Agassi can earn millions from sponsorship deals with companies, such as Nike, who are eager to associate themselves with sporting winners. However, it is generally the top-seeded players that secure such lucrative deals.

GLOSSARY

Advantage – An advantage is given to a player when he scores a point after deuce.

Ace – A serve that lands within the court boundaries without being returned.

Backspin – When the ball is struck at the bottom by the racket, causing reverse spin.

Block – A shortened stroke that uses the momentum of the ball to carry it back over the net.

Centre mark – A mark on the baseline that indicates the serving position.

Chopper grip – Another name for the continental grip.

Cross-court – The action of going diagonally across the court.

Deuce – When the score in a game is 40/40.

Double fault – When both serves fail to land in the service box.

Drive – A term used to describe a forehand or backhand groundstroke.

Fault – Any action in tennis that contravenes the rules.

Flight – The path in which the ball is travelling.

Follow-through – The natural path the racket takes after it has hit the ball.

Half volley – A volley that is played just as the ball hits the ground.

Let – When a serve hits the net but lands in the service box.

Love – The tennis equivalent to zero.

Match point – The last point that decides the winner of the match.

Net cord – A ball that hits the net as it goes over. It is only called a let when this occurs during service.

Point – What is scored at the end of a rally or single shot.

Pass – A shot that goes over an opponent at the net.

Rally – A series of shots played back and forth between players in order to win a point.

Receiver – A player who is waiting to return a ball.

Return – A shot that is played back over the net from the previous shot or serve.

Sidespin – The spin created when the racket hits the ball from left to right or right to left, causing it to bounce sideways.

Set – When a player has won six games or beaten the opponent by two clear games.

Second serve – A serve which is taken when the first one has been deemed a fault.

Slice – The racket action that puts backspin or sidespin on a ball.

Split-step – A small bounce that is made just before playing a shot.

Take-back – When the racket is taken back to hit the ball.

Topspin – The forward rotation of the ball that causes it to bounce high on landing.

Tramlines – The parallel lines of the single and double sidelines.

Underspin – When the ball is struck at the bottom causing reverse spin.

Volley – A shot played where the ball does not bounce.

Western – An exaggerated style of grip that produces topspin.

LISTINGS

ITF Licencing Ltd (International Tennis Federation)
Bank Lane, Roehampton, London SW15 5XZ, UK
Tel: +44 (0) 20 8878 6464 Fax: +44 (0) 20 8392 4747
Website: www.itftennis.com

LTA (Lawn Tennis Association)
Queens Club, Palliser Road, West Kensington, London W14 9EG, UK
Tel: +44 (0) 20 7381 7000 Fax: +44 (0) 20 7381 5965
Website: www.lta.org.uk